The Haida

JENNIFER NAULT

Weigl

Published by Weigl Educational Publishers Limited
6325 10th Street SE
Calgary, Alberta T2H 2Z9

Website: www.weigl.ca

Library and Archives Canada Cataloguing in Publication

Nault, Jennifer, author
        Haida / Jennifer Nault.

(Aboriginal art & culture)
Issued in print and electronic formats.
ISBN 978-1-4872-0236-1 (bound).--ISBN 978-1-4872-0237-8 (pbk.).--
ISBN 978-1-4872-0238-5 (ebook)

        1. Haida Indians--Juvenile literature. 1. Title.

E99.H2N33 2015   j971.1004'9728   C2015-901036-5
                                                    C2015-901037-3

Printed in the United States of America in Brainerd, Minnesota
1 2 3 4 5 6 7 8 9 19 18 17 16 15

082015
100815

Project Coordinator: Heather Kissock
Design: Terry Paulhus

Every reasonable effort has been made to trace ownership and to obtain permission to reprint copyright material. The publishers would be pleased to have any errors or omissions brought to their attention so that they may be corrected in subsequent printings.

We acknowledge the financial support of the Government of Canada through the Canada Book Fund for our publishing activities.

Weigl acknowledges Getty Images, Alamy, Corbis, Shutterstock, iStock, Thinkstock, the Qay'llnagaay Heritage Centre Society, and the Canadian Museum of History as its primary image suppliers for this title.

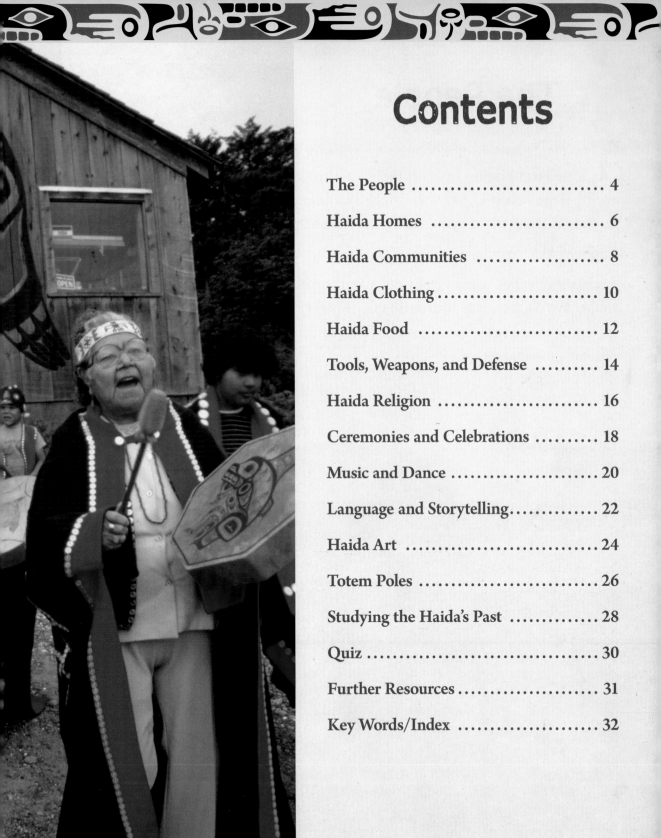

Contents

🦅 The People

The Haida have lived in North America for more than 8,000 years. This **First Nation** lives off the west coast of British Columbia on an **archipelago** called Haida Gwaii. The Haida can also be found in Alaska, on the southern tip of Prince of Wales Island. All Haida speak a distinct language also called Haida.

Archaeological evidence gives clues about the Haida's past. Their population could have once been as high as 30,000. This is based on the number of ancient sites and settlements discovered around Haida Gwaii. Most of these sites are now abandoned.

HAIDA MAP

The **traditional** lands of the Haida in Canada and the United States.

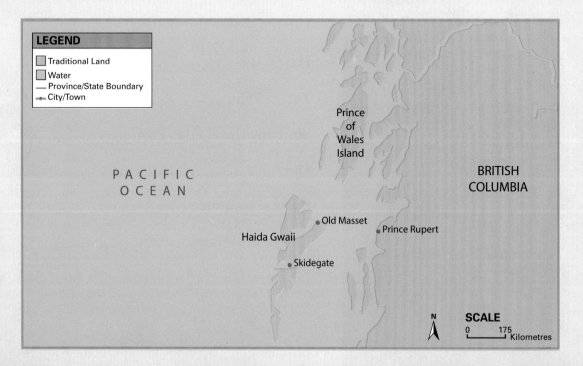

LEGEND
- Traditional Land
- Water
- Province/State Boundary
- City/Town

Prince of Wales Island

PACIFIC OCEAN

BRITISH COLUMBIA

Old Masset

Prince Rupert

Haida Gwaii

Skidegate

N

SCALE
0   175
Kilometres

When Europeans arrived in the late 1700s, the Haida had about 50 villages scattered throughout Haida Gwaii. Haida society was highly developed because their island location made it easy to thrive. The climate was warm, and they had steady access to natural resources such as trees, birds, and fish. The Haida were excellent hunters and gatherers, getting all they needed to survive from their surroundings.

The Haida built large wooden canoes for hunting, fishing, and battle. Today, they still use canoes for special occasions, such as weddings.

HAIDA GWAII

There are more than **200 islands** in the Haida Gwaii archipelago.

Haida Gwaii has a total area of **1,000,000** hectares.

The west coast of Haida Gwaii gets the strongest **winds** in Canada.

Today, there are about **4,000 Haida** living in **Canada**. Half of these people live in Haida Gwaii.

The closest city to Haida Gwaii, **Prince Rupert**, is an **8-hour ferry ride** away.

Haida Homes

The Haida lived in large cedar-plank homes called longhouses. Haida villages were made up of one or more rows of longhouses lined up along a shoreline. In the middle of the village stood the chief's house, which was larger than the others. The Haida believed that the house was one of the main gifts from Raven, who had stolen the idea from Beaver. This house was the centre of Haida life.

Different regions of Haida Gwaii had slightly different house styles. Haida houses were rectangular and were made of red cedar planks. In the northern part of Haida Gwaii, the houses were framed on the inside. In the south, the frames were on the outside. Thick corner posts supported the huge beams of wood.

Haida longhouses were all positioned to have their doorway facing the shore.

Some Haida houses had a doorway that featured a **totem pole**. The doorway was created by cutting an opening through the pole. The pole and the front of the house would be artistically carved and painted.

Usually, a Haida house had one fire pit in the centre. There were no windows, so there was a smoke hole through the roof. A board was propped up to protect the opening of the hole from leaks. An entire household shared the fire for heat and cooking. They slept near the fire on a raised platform.

The roof of a Haida longhouse was quite low, making the house easier to heat in winter. To handle the large amount of rain in the area, the roof was pitched, or downward sloping.

DWELLING AND DECORATION

An average Haida longhouse was about **33** metres **long** and **17** metres **wide**.

About **35 to 70** people shared a Haida longhouse, depending on its size.

Each family in a Haida longhouse had its own sleeping area **divided off** by **woven mats** or **planks**.

The Haida created special tools, such as **mauls**, to **build** their **houses**. Mauls were similar to **hammers**.

In the Haida chief's house, there was a **carved seat** of honour for him. Everyone else sat on boxes or mats.

Haida Communities

The Haida were divided into two social groups, or clans. One group was called Raven and the other was called Eagle. Each clan had access to special resources, such as fishing spots and land. Clans preserved their own stories, dances, and songs. Within each clan, there were smaller family groups. Marriages could only take place between Eagles and Ravens. Haida in the same clan could not marry.

Haida communities spread out over many villages, and each village had several households. A chief was in charge of each household. Most consisted of about 35 people. Some of the more powerful chiefs could command much larger households. A head chief was chosen to control the village itself.

Women in Haida villages were in charge of the home. They performed many of the household chores and kept the community in order. Haida women were accomplished weavers and sewers. They were known for their cedar-bark clothing, head coverings, and basketry.

The older generation of Haida pass on the ancient customs and traditions to the next generation.

Haida men often hunted and fished. They sometimes waged war on other First Nations of the Northwest Coast. Haida men were known as excellent warriors.

Today, the people of Haida Gwaii work in fishing, canning, and logging. Some also work in tourism. They show visitors the beauty and culture of the islands.

Haida women wove baskets and hats with cedar bark strips or with dried spruce roots.

GOVERNMENT

Today, there are two main Haida villages on Haida Gwaii. One is Skidegate, at the south end of Graham Island. The other village is Masset, at Masset Inlet. Each of these two villages has its own village council. The Council of the Haida Nation governs the two villages. The council was formed in 1974. It was created to protect the land and the rights of the Haida.

In the late 1700s, Skidegate was a centre for trading otter pelts. Today, the town lives mainly from eco-tourism and cultural activities.

Haida Clothing

Before they came in contact with Europeans, most Haida wore clothes made from red or yellow cedar bark. Strips of bark were woven to create different kinds of fabrics. Some fabrics were soft, while others were dense and waterproof. The Haida decorated many articles of clothing with family crest figures relating to the two clans, Eagle and Raven. The family crest was often displayed on carved wooden head ornaments, called frontlets. Frontlets were sewn or tied onto a headdress made from strips of bark or baleen.

A beautifully carved frontlet would be one of a Haida's most prized possessions.

Women wore skirts and capes. In cool weather, men wore leggings, woven aprons, tunics, and capes. Capes were made of elkskin or of cedar bark woven with mountain goat wool. Both men and women wore broad-brimmed hats woven from spruce roots to protect their eyes from the sun.

Chiefs wore special clothing, such as capes lined with sea otter fur and decorated with crest figures. For special ceremonies, chiefs wore elaborate headdresses.

After they started trading furs with the Europeans, the Haida began to wear the blankets they received in exchange. Blankets were wrapped around the body during the day and used to keep warm at night.

Traditionally, Haida women wove the hats, and Haida men decorated them with animal designs.

MASKS

The Haida wore masks for special ceremonies, **potlatch** performances, and **pole raisings**. Special masks were also worn by dancers in secret societies. Secret societies were an important feature of Haida culture. To become a member, one had to go through **initiation rites** to gain the protection of a powerful guardian spirit. The masks were believed to give the dancers the power to communicate with the spirit world.

Haida masks were usually made of wood or copper. They could be decorated with paint, bark, leather, or fur.

🦅 Haida Food

Being so close to the Pacific Ocean made it easy for the Haida to find food. Salmon was one of their main food sources. Since there was no refrigeration, the Haida had to **preserve** most of the salmon. They did this by hanging it over a fire and smoking it.

The Haida ate other ocean fish as well, including halibut, cod, smelt, and herring. They also hunted whale and seal. On land, the Haida hunted deer, elk, moose, beaver, and other animals. Everybody in the village helped with hunting and fishing.

The Haida also gathered cranberries, huckleberries, and other berries that were in season. They were preserved in bottles of whale or seal oil. Seaweed was collected and dried. The Haida also ate the shoots or roots of many other plants.

Food was often cooked in bentwood boxes. To make the boxes, sheets of cedar bark were steamed, bent, and joined at the corners. The boxes were filled with water. Then, heated rocks were added to boil the food in the box.

Apart from fish and clams, the Haida ate dried herring eggs on seaweed. K'aaw, as it is called, is a highly prized speciality today.

Haida Halibut Soup

Ingredients:

- 4 large potatoes
- 1/2 onion
- 1 kilogram of halibut, cubed
- 1 1/2 cups evaporated milk
- 1 can cream of celery soup (undiluted)
- pepper to taste
- water

Equipment:

- cutting knife
- cooking pot
- stove
- fork

Directions:

1. With an adult's help, chop the potatoes and onions, and place them in a pot.

2. Add water to cover the potatoes. Boil until the potatoes are tender.

3. Reduce the heat to medium. Add the halibut, and cook until a fork goes into the fish easily.

4. Add the milk and soup. Simmer for 5 minutes.

5. Add pepper to taste.

Tools, Weapons, and Defense

The Haida developed a number of useful tools and weapons for fishing and hunting. The women wove special basket traps for catching fish. Fishers also used rakes, weirs, hooks, lines, and spears. Rakes were large forks made of wood or bone that were fastened to wooden poles. Weirs were fence-like structures that were stretched across a stream. Fish would swim into the weirs and get caught in them.

The Haida were known as strong warriors. They were feared by other **Aboriginal** groups along the coast, including the Tlingit and the Tsimshian. Battles often took place at sea. To transport themselves, the Haida used their vast supply of giant western red cedar trees to make large canoes. Each canoe was carved from a single cedar tree. Some of these canoes could fit up to 60 paddlers.

Haida carvers continue the art of carving canoes out of a single tree today.

Haida warriors were equipped for battle. They wore armour, helmets, and thick war coats. For weapons, they used bows and arrows and spears. Sometimes, heavy stone rings were tied to ropes and hurled at enemy vessels. The stones could then be pulled back and used again. War daggers were also used during both land and sea raids.

Haida war helmets were designed to look like the head of an animal, such as a seal.

HUNTING AND CARVING TOOLS

Haida fishhooks were made out of bone or wood. Fishline was made out of cedar bark.

The Haida made woodworking tools out of hardwood, shells, bones, and horns.

The Haida used sandstones for sharpening tools. They used sharkskins for sanding wood.

To split wood, the Haida used sledgehammers made out of stone.

The Haida hunted animals such as sea otters from their canoes using bows and arrows.

Haida Religion

The Haida believed that all things, living and non-living, had a spirit. They respected animals as their equals and believed in treating all of nature with great respect. It was important to be thankful for nature's resources. For instance, ceremonies were performed to give thanks before hunting, fishing, or cutting down a tree.

In Haida society, shamans, or medicine people, were the link between the spirit world and the natural world. Shamans were helped by **supernatural** beings whose powers came from nature. Male shamans usually dealt with trading and warfare. Female shamans cured illnesses and helped with childbirth.

Shamans wore special jewellery and clothes, such as a Chilkat, or dancing blanket, during ceremonies.

The Haida believed that a person's illness could be caused by losing their soul. It was the shaman's responsibility to retrieve the lost soul from the spirit world and return it to the sick person. The shaman used a carved, hollow bone called a soul-catcher to capture the lost soul and keep it until it could be returned to its owner. Shamans used other **sacred** items in their healing ceremonies, as well.

Shamans often used rattles and charms to connect with the spirit world.

THE SPIRIT WORLD

For the Haida, the spirit world resembled the real world. Animals were a respected part of the spirit world and held deep spiritual meaning. The spirit world was organized much like their own society. The supernatural beings resided in one of three worlds. The sky was the upper world. Haida Gwaii was the land world. Below it was the sea world, on which the entire coastline of British Columbia rested.

According to Haida legend , the islands of Haida Gwaii were created when the world was still covered with water.

Ceremonies and Celebrations

The two Haida clans of Eagle and Raven are often depicted on mortuary poles and grave markers.

The Haida held many kinds of ceremonies. In Haida society, high-ranking people, such as chiefs, organized dance performances, feasts, and potlatches. Potlatches were the most important of these events. They were generally held to mark a special occasion, such as the birth or death of a noble person, or to exchange goods. A potlatch was an opportunity for a chief to display wealth and **social status**.

When a noble person died, a **mortuary** potlatch was held, and a mortuary pole was raised. At this event, the **title** of the deceased was passed on to the heir, usually the next oldest brother. The belongings of the deceased were given to relatives. The Haida did not always see death as a sad event. They believed in reincarnation, or rebirth. People close to death would sometimes even choose their next parents.

Completing a longhouse was also a reason for celebration. Houses took great effort to build and decorate. The new house owner gave a large potlatch to thank those involved in building the house.

Potlatches also helped to maintain good relations between villages, clans, and Aboriginal groups. A very big potlatch might take years to plan and last several days. At the end, gifts would be distributed to the guests. The higher the rank of the guest, the more valuable their gift would be.

Haida mortuary poles from the 19th century are now part of a UNESCO World Heritage site.

POTLATCHES

The missionaries and government officials of the past did not understand the cultural value of the potlatches. They did not think it was good for the chiefs to give away so much of their wealth. They worried that diseases would spread more quickly at the huge gatherings. The government banned potlatches from 1884 to 1951. Today, potlatches are once again a part of Haida society.

Today, potlatches are held to celebrate occasions such as weddings, baby showers, and graduations.

🦅 Music and Dance

Ceremonial headdresses were worn for occasions such as welcome dances.

Dance has always been an important part of Haida culture. Many dances feature shamans, chiefs, and members of secret societies, but other members of the community dance as well. Dancers wear clothing and masks to represent different characters.

One dance was only performed by men of the Ulala society. The signal that the dancers were about to make their entrance was given by spinning a pole that had cedar bark streamers hanging from it. Other important dances were the Eagle Dance, the Raven Dance, and the Salmon Dance.

By the 1870s, Haida dances were taking place less often. Europeans did not understand Haida dancing and felt threatened by it. They tried to prevent it. However, the Haida continued to dance in secret.

The Haida continue to teach their songs to younger generations to ensure that their traditions live on.

DRUMMING AND SONGS

The Haida made music with drums, rattles, and their voices. Drums were made by stretching animal skin tightly across a circular wooden frame. The drumstick consisted of a wooden stick with a leather-padded tip.

Rattles were used to lure the salmon to Haida villages. The swishing sound they made sounded like salmon fins moving through the water.

Haida songs told complex stories. They could be about love, war, birth, or death, or were simply to give thanks.

In the 1960s, there were fewer than 30 Haida **elders** left who still knew the traditional songs. Since the 1970s, there has been a resurgence of Haida music.

Haida drummers take part in many festivals in Canada.

Language and Storytelling

Before Europeans came to the land, the Haida language thrived. Today, few speakers of the Haida language remain, and most are seniors. The Haida people will lose much of their **oral** history if they lose their language, so they are working hard to preserve it. In schools, teachers are making the Haida language part of daily lessons. They invite elders into the classroom to share the language through songs and prayers.

Some Haida speakers in Canada are taking part in a special program to preserve the language. They are recording the language for future generations.

Different Haida villages spoke slightly different dialects. Today, three dialects are left. The Southern and Northern dialects are both spoken on Haida Gwaii. The Kaigani dialect is spoken by Haida who live in Alaska.

Like many Aboriginal groups, the Haida shared knowledge through storytelling. They have many stories to explain **creation** and how the world works. Raven is one of the most important creatures in Haida myth. Raven is a trickster, but he teaches people how to live a proper life.

One story tells how the first people were born from a huge clamshell on the beach. The people were afraid to leave the shell, but Raven helped them out of the shell so they could live on this Earth. Many other stories tell how Raven brought useful items to humans, such as fresh water or salmon.

MONTHS

The names of the months in the Southern Haida dialect reflect the Haida's close connection to nature.

January — Taan Kung
Bear Moon

March — Hlgidᴳun Kʼah Kung
Laughing Geese Month

July — Ԍaanᴳaalansdll Kung
Ripe Berries Month

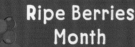

August — Chiina Kung
Salmon Moon

November — Chaaᴳan Kung
Bear Hibernate Month

December — Taada Kung
Ice Moon

🦅 Haida Art

Everything the Haida made was created with skill and precision and beautifully decorated. Even simple household objects were often works of art. The Haida are renowned for a style of decoration known as flat design. It used black outlines to create flowing forms and bright colors, often red, to fill the spaces inside the lines. Totem poles, masks, and houses were all decorated in this style.

Haida items were also often decorated with spiritual images and crests. Crests showed figures of animals, birds, and sea creatures linked to a family's heritage and to related myths. Supernatural beings were depicted as well. It took many years to become a skilled artist or master carver.

The Haida decorated not only clothing and jewellery, but also practical items such as tools and storage boxes.

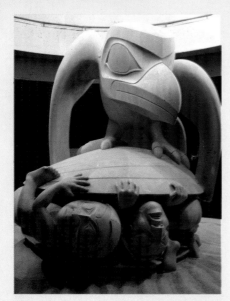

One of Bill Reid's most famous sculptures is based on the Haida creation story of *The Raven and the First Men.*

The Haida traded with Europeans and other Aboriginal groups for materials and resources they did not have. They began to use these mineral **pigments**, stones, and metals in their works of art.

Today, Haida art is valued around the world. One of the first Haida artists to draw the attention of the art world was Bill Reid. Reid started to gain acclaim as a sculptor and painter in the late 1900s. Robert Davidson, who followed in Reid's footsteps, is another gifted Haida artist with an international reputation.

EUROPEAN CONTACT

When Europeans brought new art techniques and materials to their land, the Haida began to experiment with them. They developed new designs that were sometimes quite different from traditional ones. They made small carvings of **argillite**, ivory, and silver, as well as wooden and basketry pieces. Some of these small pieces of art, which were bought by Europeans, have been saved and can be found in museum collections today.

Haida artists started carving with argillite in the early 1800s.

🦅 Totem Poles

The totem pole is probably the best known Haida art form. The Haida usually carved the poles from red cedar trees. Red cedar is easy to carve and does not rot as fast as other wood. Archaeologists believe that totem pole design developed over thousands of years. They have found remnants from ancient totem poles that show similar designs to totem poles from more recent history.

The designs on totem poles can mean different things. The poles often display crests that show family connections. They may represent stories of the past, family history, or other important events. Totem poles were also carved to celebrate cultural traditions. Welcoming poles were erected near the shoreline to show ownership of the land and to welcome guests. Mortuary poles were used to honour the dead, much like a headstone is used.

Contemporary artists carve totem poles today based on traditional styles.

The figures commonly found on Haida totem poles include Raven and Eagle. Each figure has its own story to tell and may be carved in different parts of the pole. The larger a figure is, the more important it is to the story.

In the 1960s, a team of Aboriginal carvers spent four years recreating a Haida village at the University of British Columbia.

TOTEM POLES

Most totem poles were from **3** to **20** metres tall. However, on **Haida Gwaii**, some are more than **30** metres tall.

If an important chief died, his successor would raise a memorial pole for him about one year after his death.

It can take **100** or more people to carry a pole and raise it when it is completed.

Totem poles can last for about **100** years because cedar wood does not rot easily.

The Haida **stopped** carving totem poles for nearly **100 years** because the **Europeans** did not approve of them.

STUDYING THE HAIDA'S PAST

Archaeologists study items left by cultures from the past. A number of archaeologists have spent time on Haida Gwaii examining old village sites and **artifacts**. The first such visit in 1919 produced many clues to the Haida's past. Stone tools were found in **intertidal** areas that were once dry land. Old middens, which are hills of litter, were also discovered. These helped the archaeologists learn about the way the Haida once lived and what was important in their lives.

Archaeological studies show that, in prehistoric times, the Haida used tools such as hammers.

Timeline

Archaic Period

3000 B.C.—1000 B.C.

Shellfish provide the Haida's ancestors with a constant food supply. No longer needing to search for food, they settle in Haida Gwaii.

Pre-Contact Period

1000 B.C.—A.D. 1

Salmon fishing starts to become a major food source for the Haida. The Haida start to trade with neighbouring Aboriginal peoples.

European Contact

1774—1900

Spanish explorer Juan Perez arrives in Haida Gwaii. Soon, European gold miners and traders are visiting regularly. By 1900, Europeans have settled the area.

There is still much to learn. However, archaeological research must be done with caution. There are ancient burial grounds, for example, that should not be disturbed. For this reason, any research must be done in consultation with Haida experts.

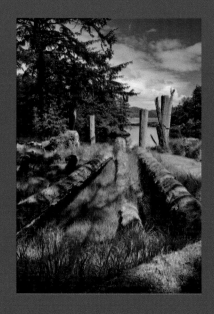

The remains of a Haida longhouse can give archaeologists clues about ancient Haida dwellings and villages.

Population Decline

1900—1960

By 1915, the population of Haida Gwaii has been reduced to fewer than 600 people by diseases, such as smallpox. Much of the Haida's oral history and tradition is lost.

Cultural Revival

1960s—present

The Haida start to revive their ancient traditions and customs. Haida culture flourishes and Haida art gains respect around the world.

Haida Enterprise Corporation

2009

The Haida Nation launches an organization to support Haida businesses and **sustainable** growth.

QUIZ

1 What do the Haida of Canada call the group of islands where they live?

A. Haida Gwaii

2 What is the most important ceremony for the Haida?

A. The potlatch

3 In what kind of home did the Haida live?

A. A longhouse

4 The Haida built their canoes out of which trees?

A. Western red cedar trees

5 What natural material did Haida women use to weave clothing and basketry?

A. Cedar bark and dried spruce roots

6 What are the two clans of the Haida called?

A. Raven and Eagle

7 How many dialects of the Haida language are there?

A. Three

8 What is the name of the Haida's main style of decoration?

A. Flat design

9 What was the traditional main food source of the Haida?

A. Salmon

10 When did the Haida first come into contact with Europeans?

A. 1774

FURTHER RESOURCES

BOOKS

Read an interesting review of Haida culture in **Haida: Their Art and Culture** by Leslie Drew (Big Country Books, 1983).

There are countless books on Haida Gwaii for people visiting the area. For a visitor's account, read **Haida Gwaii: The Queen Charlotte Islands** by Dennis Horwood and Tom Parkin (Heritage House, 2009).

WEBSITES

To find out more about the Haida and their way of life, visit the following websites. Other reputable websites usually include government sites, educational sites, and online encyclopedias.

Read about the children of Eagle and Raven at the Canadian Museum of History at www.historymuseum.ca/cmc/exhibitions/aborig/haida/haindexe.shtml

Learn about the Haida language at www.haidanation.ca/Pages/language/skidegate.html

See a collection of photos, both old and new, of life in Haida Gwaii at www.virtualmuseum.ca/virtual-exhibits/exhibit/haida-memories/

KEY WORDS

Aboriginal: original inhabitants of a country

archaeological: relating to the study of objects from the past to learn about people who lived long ago

archipelago: a group of islands

argillite: a soft black rock used in Haida sculpture

artifacts: items, such as tools, made by humans in the past

creation: the forming of the universe and all its inhabitants

elders: the older and more influential people of a group or community

First Nation: a member of Canada's Aboriginal community who is not Inuit or Métis

initiation rites: ceremonies and tasks a person undergoes to be admitted into a group or society

intertidal: beach area that is underwater at high tide

mortuary: relating to burial

oral: spoken, not written

pigments: colouring material used as paint or dye

pole raisings: the placement of totem poles in an upright position after the carving is completed

potlatch: Haida ceremony involving feasting, gift-giving, and dancing

preserve: process food, for example, by salting, smoking, or drying, to keep it from spoiling

sacred: worthy of religious worship

social status: ranking within a community

supernatural: a force existing outside the laws of nature

sustainable: using resources in such a way that they do not become depleted

title: proper name, often giving status

totem pole: a large, upright pole that is carved and painted with First Nations emblems

traditional: to do with established beliefs or practices

INDEX